35 Pooping Positions to Spice Up the Bathroom

By G.A. James

Copyright © 2015 G.A. James

All rights reserved.

DISCLAIMER

The author is not responsible for any emotional or bodily injury resulting from the following advice

#1 - The Arm Wrestler

A little healthy competition can be a great way to find relief when backed up

#2 - Side Saddle

Perfect for the wide-bottomed pooper

#3 - Sit-Up

Your abs won't be the only thing burning

#4 – The Cradle

Great for the extra messy ones

#5 – Monkey See, Monkey Do-Do

Gives Ape Sh*$ a whole new meaning

#6 - The Hovercrap

Zero contact. Just a clean lean.

#7 - Skydumping

The most expensive way to poop and the most thrilling

#8 - The Lunge

Great thigh workout. No clean-up. Heroic.

#9 - The Vain Strain

Look at yourself, pooping has never looked so good.

#10 - The Tea Potty

Would you like one dump or two with that?

#11 - The Backdrop

Also known as The Bar Stool

#12 - The Rocket

3.....2.....1.....BLAST OFF!

#13 - The Sleeper

Lay back and get some rest. You won't even know you went.

#14 - Second Down

A great trick for dinner parties

#15 - The Meditator

Inhale through the nose, long exhale through the mouth

#16 - The Slam Deuce

RUN   JUMP   SLAM!

Best for padded seats

#17 - Too Cool For Stool

Deny it all you want

#18 - The Aristocrap

I'm ready Alfred...

#19 - The Olympian

Balance. Concentration. Defecation.

#20 - The Turdle

Slow and Painful

#21 - The Royal Throne

Nobody craps higher than a king

#22 - Toilet Trash

Not recommended for public restrooms

#23 – Maximum Comfart

for those who have all the time in the world

#24 – The Whoopsie

Maybe next time

#25 - Mobowel Movement

Fully equipped with a pedal-activated flusher and a speed bump-activated bidet

#26 - The DUMPster Dive

Like a bird bath for humans

#27 - The Dove Dropping

Be sure to hold on to the thicker branches

#28 - The Magician

And now for my final trick...

#29 - Loud and Proud

Turn up the bass, this one's a doozy

#30 - The Bookworm

Everything sounds better on paper. To wipe, all you have to do is wiggle.

#31 - The Bumbadeer

Those circular butt-sized windows are begging to be pooped out of

#32 - In the Hood

Totally gangster and the warmest seat in the house

#33 - The "I Quit" Sh#$

Go out with a bang

#34 – The Floater

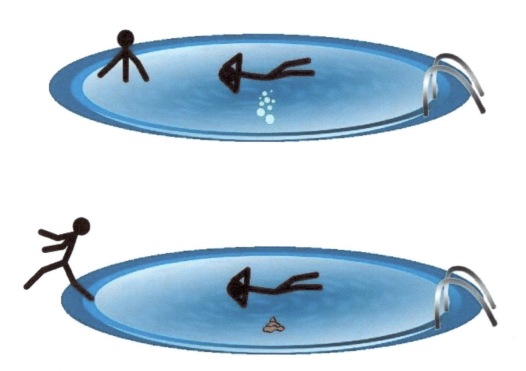

Pools are giant toilets you can relax in

#35 - Dream Come Poo

Go back to bed, it can wait.

HAPPY POOPING!

ABOUT THE AUTHOR: G.A. James is a professional pooper of 25 years and has been changing lives across the globe with his unique art form and technique. By his early twenties, James had experienced two colonoscopies, a sphincterotomy, and countless anal fissures. Now he wants to bring his talents to your toilet.

Printed in the USA
CPSIA information can be obtained
at www.ICGtesting.com
LVHW070615271023
762200LV00034B/25